Everything you need to know about

FORMULA 1
2022

MELVIN WEZENBERG

To achieve anything in this game, you must be prepared to dabble in the boundary of disaster.
Stirling Moss

PROLOGUE

Formula 1. Some call it the elite of motor sport, some call it Netflix's greatest reality show. However, you view it, the fact that you purchased this book indicates that you're interested enough to learn more about the sport.

I've been a Formula 1 watcher since 2010 but started to truly understand all the rules, teams, drivers, and tech since 2016. This year, more and more of my friends, family and colleagues started watching Formula 1. While Formula 1 is very entertaining to watch (especially the 2021 season), certain races involved a lot of incidents that required knowledge about Formula 1 to fully enjoy the races. I got a lot of questions and calls from friends asking me to explain what was currently happening on the screen and why certain decisions were made. Why was Max given a 5-place grid penalty after the Monza incident? When can drivers replace their engines without getting a penalty? Why did Max get a 20-grid place penalty when he replaced his engine but Lewis and Valtteri (Bottas) only received 5? What happens under a red safety flag? And how come we had half points this season? Why was Shaquille O'Neill suddenly on the podium? I want to take the time to explain all of these questions and give everyone the full updates on what happened last season and how this may impact and continue this season. I hope you enjoy this book, but even more so, I hope this book lets you enjoy Formula 1 Season 2022!

(TW/rrando19)
    Photoshopped image of Shaquille O'Neill on Formula 1 podium at the U.S. Grand Prix

CHAPTER 0

INTRODUCTION TO FORMULA 1 AND A BRIEF MODERN HISTORY

If you have been watching Formula 1 (F1) steadily for multiple seasons now, you can skip this chapter as its meant to introduce some more basic topics for those who only started following the sport recently. Formula 1 was established in 1950 with some of the first races held at Silverstone (United Kingdom), Monaco (City Race), Spa (Belgium) and Monza (Italy). Because these tracks have been around since the beginning, they are often viewed as the "classic" tracks of the sport and races there tend to be seen as the special races of the season. The very first Formula 1 World Championship was won by Giuseppe Farina in an Alpha Romeo and while the sport has since seen winners, teams and drivers from all over the world, it is still a sport that lives very much in the heart of many Italians. The current form of the top car racing sport in the world is quite complex and has a lot of terminology that comes up regularly. Therefore, in order to make the rest of this book easier to understand, we'll go ahead and describe how Formula 1 has looked especially in the last decade.

In the last couple of years, Formula 1 consists of 10 teams competing each with 2 drivers summing up to a total of 20 cars on track. While women are allowed to compete, we have only seen men compete in more recent years in Formula 1 (but women have been racing in the other division of the sport like the W Series, Formula 3 and Formula Renault.) The 10 teams that are currently competing in Formula 1 (in order of their finishing position) are:

1. Mercedes
2. Red Bull
3. Ferarri
4. Mclaren
5. Alpine
6. Alpha Tauri
7. Aston Martin
8. Williams
9. Alpha Romeo
10. Haas

Like in most sports, there have been several era's of supremacy by certain teams. You can compare it to Real Madrid winning the Champions League three years in a row between 2016 and 2018, or Nadal winning the French Open 5 years in a row. The latest dominances have been held by Red Bull Racing (winning between 2010-2014) and Mercedes (winning everything after 2014). However, last season the sport became extremely interesting as the 7-time world champion Lewis Hamilton was challenged by the young talent Max Verstappen. Some other details to know about the teams in F1 is that Ferrari holds an honorary spot in the sport. To say Formula 1 without Ferrari would be like Major League Baseball without the New York Yankees doesn't even cut it as Ferrari has been a part of Formula 1 since the very creation of F1. Ferrari is the sport's most prestigious team, having won the most races and championships, by far. Thanks to this, Ferrari tends to get a couple of extra benefits that other teams do not get and beyond that most drivers dream to drive for Ferrari at some point in their careers, regardless of the current performance of the team. Almost as famous as Ferrari are Micheal Schumacher and Lewis Hamilton, whom are currently tied for the all time record for most won championships at 7 titles each.

Formula 1 is owned by the Liberty Media Corporation and generates a net income of over 2.67 billion dollars every year. That money gets split 50-50 between the competing F1 Teams and the Formula 1 Group. There are two championships happening in an F1 Season; The Drivers Championship and the Constructors (Teams) championships. Only the constructor's championship provides price money, while the driver's championship is for honour. Last year Mercedes (1st place) earned over 700 million dollars while Red Bull (2nd place) "only" earned 165 million. The FIA can be seen as the FIFA in Football or the ITF in Tennis, and is the governing body of the sport- updating rules and enforcing penalties. Just like a player can get a yellow or red card in Football, drivers can also get penalties for driving too aggressive or not following the rules. Teams in F1 can also be punished for any rule break that may occur throughout a season. In the 2020 season, one of the teams had clearly copied the car off another team and therefore breached the rules. They were punished by the FIA and lost half of their points earned throughout the season. For the sake of making this as easy to understand, the most important person in the

FIA last year was Michael Massi as he controlled the in-race communication between teams and the race stewards. The race stewards are equal to the referees of the race and change every race. There are usually 3 to 4 race stewards per race. Micheal Massi would have the power to negotiate penalties with teams last year, and this resulted in several controversial calls being made throughout the season. As a result of this, Michael Massi has been replaced by two others; Niels Wittich and Eduardo Freitas. There will also be a VAR equivalent in F1 this year, based in Geneva, that will monitor any decision made by the referees and if seen unfair, can be overthrown. Now let's create a quick team sheet to help you understand all important characters in F1.

CHEAT SHEET

SCUDERIA   FERRARI

Scuderia Ferrari is also called the "Prancing Horse" and is led by team principle Mattia Binotto. While they have an amazing history, they have struggled in recent years. 2022 pre-season testing shows they look to have a strong year in 2022 which would be great for the Ferrari brand. Their driver lineup consists of Charles Leclerc from Monaco and Carlos Sainz Jr. from Spain. Charles is seen as the super talent that will carry Ferrari back to their glory days and he has signed a contract until 2025 with the

2021

2022

Micheal Massi   **Niels Wittich**   **Eduardo Freitas**

team. Carlos Sainz joined the team last season and has shown that he is able to match the talent of Charles Leclerc. Carlos Sainz continues his family's legacy as his dad was also a Formula 1 driver. The Ferrari fans are commonly referred to as the Tifosi and they are some of the most passionate fans in

  F1. While Alpha Tauri is another
Italian based team, it is Scuderia

Scuderia　　**Mattia**　　　**Charles**　　　**Carlos**
Ferrari　　　**Binotto**　　　**Leclerc**　　　**Sainz Jr.**

Ferrari that is seen as the
main Italian team competing in F1.

Toto Wolff **Lewis Hamilton** **George Russel**

MERCEDES AMG PETRONAS F1 TEAM

Merceds AMG Petronas F1 Team is also called the "Silver Arrows" and is led by team principle Toto Wolff. Toto Wolff is seen as one of the most successful team leads in Formula 1 history as he has dominated the sport ever since he took over at Mercedes. Wolff is not only the team boss but actually owns 33% of Mercedes F1, making him one of three owners (the others are Daimler and Ineos). His success in Formula 1 has not only shown in his several achievements over the years but also in his net worth, totalling at $580 million (which is more than double that of star driver Lewis Hamilton). Together with Lewis Hamilton the team has been almost unbeatable over the last 8 years. They are incredibly quick and Lewis is seen as the world's best driver today. This year, Valterri Bottas has been replaced by George Russel, giving the Mercedes team 2 British drivers. George Russel was previously at Williams and has been with the Mercedes Youth academy for a long time now. Historically, Lewis Hamilton was seen as the "first" driver, with Valterri as a strategic second driver. Now with George Russel joining the team we will yet have to see how the dynamics between the two drivers will be this year.

Red Bull Racing   **Christian Horner**   **Max Verstappen**   **Checo Perez**

RED BULL RACING

Red Bull Racing is led by team principle Christian Horner. When talking about successful team bosses, Christian Horner should absolutely be on your list. He led the supremacy of Red Bull between 2010 and 2014 and recruited Max Verstappen to join the team when Max was only 16 years old. Max Verstappen holds the record for youngest ever Formula 1 Driver, youngest ever Formula 1 Race winner and most paid driver together with Lewis Hamilton. Max is the current World Champion and will be driving with the number 1 this season on his car because of this. Checo Perez is an extremely experienced F1 driver from Mexico and is backed by multi-millionaire Carlos Slim. He is nicknamed "Mexico's minister of defence" after his impressive defence against Lewis Hamilton in the Abu Dhabi GP which may have cost Hamilton his championship. (We'll go into this more in the chapter on Season 2021 recap)

McLaren Racing **Zak Brown** **Lando Norris** **Daniel Ricciardo**

MCLAREN RACING

McLaren Racing is led by CEO Zak Brown since 2018, a point in which McLaren was seriously struggling with their performance. Since Brown joined the team they have been in an upward trend and have rebranded to a young and fun team. They did this also by signing young and talented driver Lando Norris from F2 in 2018. He has since become a multi-podium racer with the team and was part of the reason that McLaren finished 3rd in 2020. Last season, McLaren managed to sign Formula 1 Icon Daniel Ricciardo and while he struggled a little bit in the beginning he also won the only race for McLaren last season. Together this dynamic duo is really making McLaren a team to watch for 2022, if the car performs well!

Alpha Tauri   **Franz Tost**   Pierre Gasly   Yuki Tsunoda

ALPHA TAURI

Alpha Tauri is the new name for the sister team of Red Bull. Most people still think of this team as Toro Rosso, which is Italian for Red Bull. The name Toro Rosso got replaced by Alpha Tauri in 2020 as Red Bull wanted to promote its clothing brand in F1. Alpha Tauri is the sister team of Red Bull racing and is historically known to have the Junior drivers of Red Bull in the team. Alpha Tauri currently has ex-Red Bull driver Pierre Gasly who has really been giving Alpha Tauri extraordinary results over the last two years. Next to the frenchman, the other driver in Alpha Tauri is Japanese Yuki Tsunoda who had tied relationships with Honda. Honda was the engine supplier for both Red Bull and Alpha Tauri until 2021 and will continue to have a close relationship with the two teams from 2022 onwards even though Red Bull has purchased the engine division of Honda F1. Franz Tost is the lead of the team and is often seen to be the decision maker of who goes to Red Bull if a driver seat opens up.

Alpine F1 Team Otmar Szafnauer Fernando Alonso Estaban Ocon

ALPINE F1 TEAM

Prepare yourself for a lot of information! Alpine is a team that has got a lot of background info and recent changes. Let's start with the team name. Alpine, previously known as Renault Racing, is a team that is partly state owned and therefore is seen as the French team. Renault has been in F1 for many years and has won multiple world championships, including two with Fernando Alonso, their current driver. Fernando Alonso said goodbye to the F1 sport in 2018 when he departed from McLaren. However, he came back to Renault because he felt like he could still win more in Formula 1. He is one of the few drivers on the grid that has also won the 24hour of le mans, which makes him the second driver in history that can potentially win the Monaco GP, F1 World Championship, 24 Hours of le mans and the Indianapolis 500- also known as the triple crown. He uses the car number 14 because it has been his lucky number since his world karting championship victory where he drove with number 14, at the age of 14, on 14 July. His teammate is French driver Estaban Ocon who was forced out of his old team Force India, which was at the time ran by the newly-hired team boss of Alpine: Otmar Szafnauer. It will be interesting to see how this trio will work together this season as all of them have their unique story and history.

Aston Martin Formula 1 Team   **Mike Krack**   **Sebastian Vettel**   **Lance Stroll**

ASTON MARTIN FORMULA 1 TEAM

Aston Martin, as a company, went from being the title sponsor of Red Bull (as Aston Martin Red Bull Racing) to becoming their competition. Aston Martin went through a difficult financial period and was luckily saved by Lawrence Stroll in 2020 when he bought the company. Since Lawrence Stroll already owned the F1 Team Racing Point, he decided to merge the two companies and create Aston Martin Formula 1 Team. Luckily for Lawrence Stroll, it wasn't too hard for him to find good drivers as he has his own son Lance Stroll ready to take a seat. Lance Stroll had previously been with Williams and Racing Point and while he had some rough first seasons he has over the years proven himself as a worthy F1 Driver. His teammate is Sebastian Vettel, a four-time world champion who is slowly making his way towards the end of his career. He was booted from Ferrari to make room for Carlos Sainz and for a little bit it looked like that's where his career as driver was ending until Aston Martin took him on. Mike Krack is the new head of the team and this will be his first season in F1. He comes in as he replaced Otmar Szafnauer who is now at Alpine after Aston Martin was disappointed with his performance.

WILLIAMS RACING

Williams Racing   Simon Roberts   Alex Albon   Nicolas Latifi

WILLIAMS RACING

For British F1 fans, this team is probably a name that gives goose bumps as they were seen as the British rival of Ferrari. Between the 1980's and 2000's Williams was able to secure 9 constructor's championships and 7 driver's championships (only Ferrari has won the constructor's championship more times. 15 times, to be exact.) .Williams was an independent racing team established by Sir Frank Williams and is the only English non car -manufacturing on the grid. Unfortunately, the team had gone through some financial troubles recently and the team had to replace Claire Williams with new team lead Simon Roberts. They have had an amazing history in F1 but have seen a detrimental fall in the last decade. With their glory days in the past, this team has been making its way back up the packing order in the last year as they went from last to 8th. This year, ex Red Bull Racing driver Alex Albon joins the team and will be the only Thai driver on the grid. Next to him is Canadian Nicolas Latifi who has been with the team for a couple of years now. Williams hopes to continue fighting its way back up to the top of the grid and relive its glory days. Unfortunately, Sir Frank Williams passed away last year after a long battle with illness.

Haas F1 Team   **Guenther Steiner**   **Mick Schumacher**   **Kevin Magnussen**

HAAS F1 TEAM

Haas F1 Team is the only American team on the grid and is a small independent team. They joined F1 only very recently and performed amazingly in their first couple of years. This was against all odds as they had only minimum resources and were completely new to the sport. The main man in charge who managed to achieve this was Guenther Steiner, the most famous man in Netflix's series Drive to Survive. Since 2021, the team got a new title sponsor from Russia that had given them extra budget and new team colours. However, as Russia invaded Ukraine in February 2022, the team decided to cut all connections with the sponsor. This also meant that one of their drivers, whose family was closely linked to the sponsor, was cut and replaced with Kevin Magnussen. Kevin is a fierce driver, having scored over 158 points throughout his career. However, he's also known as an aggressive driver that will put his elbows out to overtake someone. Mick Schumacher is the driver that completes the story at Haas. He is the son of F1 Legend Michael Schumacher and will be going into his second season in F1 in 2022. The team has spent all of their time and money last season to prepare their car for 2022 and is hoping that this will be a very successful season for them.

Alpha Romeo Racing

Frédéric Vasseur

Valterri Bottas

Zhou Guanyu

ALPHA ROMEO RACING

While inherently you may think that Alpha Romeo is yet another Italian team, the truth is that Alpha Romeo actually competes under the Swiss flag. Alpha Romeo and Sauber joint forces a couple of years ago and agreed to race under the Alpha Romeo name but continued using the factory and base in Switzerland. Both Alpha Romeo and Sauber have a long history in F1 and with the very respected Frédéric Vasseur as the man in charge the team is looking at how they can move their team to become more competitive. Their driver lineup for the 2022 season holds Valterri Bottas and Zhou Guanyu. Valterri Bottas is an ex-Mercedes and ex-Williams driver that has won multiple races but never managed to win a World Championship yet. He will be bringing a lot of knowledge and experience from Mercedes to the team. The other Alpha Romeo Racing driver is Zhou Guanyu, a brand new talent in Formula 1. He will be the only Chinese driver this year and is seen as a big talent with plenty of potential to show this season.

CHAPTER 1

2021 SEASON RECAP AND LINGERING STORYLINES

Max Verstappen became the first Dutch Formula 1 Champion in History.

We all know how the season ended, with 108 million viewers it was the most viewed sporting event of 2021, a year that contained not only the Euro2020 but also the Olympics! The final race, and overall the whole season, was exhilarating with many controversies that will be remembered through history, but how did it all start? Let's go back all the way to pre-season 2021.

We started the season in Bahrain this year due to the Covid-19 Pandemic preventing the regular season start in Melbourne, Australia. But even ahead of the long awaited season-start a lot of things were happening in the driver's market that ended up having a big impact on the season. We saw Formula 1 champion Fernando Alonso's return to the sport with Alpine (previously known as Renault) as Daniel Ricciardo moved to McLaren to replace Carlos Sainz. Carlos, in turn, moved to Ferrari where he replaced Vettel as he moved to Aston Martin. With Vettel joining Aston Martin, Sergio Perez was forced to look for a new seat and found it in Red Bull Racing as Max's teammate which ultimately meant a temporary exit for Alexander Albon (he will return with Williams in 2022). If that wasn't enough to get your head spinning, McLaren had just switched engines from Renault to Mercedes while Honda announced they were to leave Formula 1 at the end of the season. (We will cover what this means for Red Bull and Alpha Tauri later) Finally, we also had three new drivers enter Formula 1 in Haas and Alpha Tauri.

Driver Changes 2021

Having all these driver and engine changes take place would eventually have a huge impact on the season. McLaren switching to Mercedes meant they were stronger than ever on the high-speed circuits. Tracks like Monza, which are known for their extremely long straights are usually won by

Mercedes or Ferrari who have the highest top speeds. However, this year the team that won in Monza was McLaren , showing the huge improvement gained by the Mercedes engine (P1. Ricciardo, P2. Norris).

So let's get going with a quick recap of the season of 2021:

The 2021 pre-season testing was held in Bahrain as F1 wanted to minimise travelling for teams during the COVID-19 pandemic. During pre-season testing a lot of data had all of the media gossiping with speculations of how this season was going to look but the gist of it was:

F1 2021 PRE-SEASON 'THE BEST SINCE RED BULL EXISTS' - MOTORSPORT.COM

LEWIS HAMILTON ADMITS MERCEDES STRUGGLES DURING PRE-SEASON TESTING- THE GUARDIAN

THE HOPES AND FEARS FOR EVERY ASTON MARTIN FAN IN 2021- FORMULA1.COM

FERNANDO ALONSO HAS NO FITNESS QUIBBLES- FORMULA1.COM

As you can tell from these newspaper headlines there are several storylines going on even before the season began. As these stories continued throughout the season, we will cover them one by one in this book. The following storylines will be covered:

1. **VER**stappen in Red Bull vs **HAM**ilton in Mercedes
2. Ferarri vs McLaren
3. Alpha Tauri vs Alpine

VERSTAPPEN AND RED BULL VS HAMILTON AND MERCEDES

Already during pre-season testing, we started to see a difference in comparison to previous years. Whereas Mercedes had always been the dominant team, this year they had some significant problems in pre-season testing and drivers were sounding nervous over their radios. Meanwhile, Red Bull seemed to be off to a flying start. With expectations for a competitive season, Formula 1 2021 kicked off with Race 1 in Bahrain. The whole weekend showed Mercedes and Red Bull being extremely competitive with one another. The weekend came to a conclusion with Verstappen taking pole position but Hamilton winning the race after Verstappen had to hand back a position for leaving the track and gaining an advantage (As stated in the F1 Rules, a drive cannot overtake outside of the track). It was the start of a season that would see a lot of these kind of regulations being enforced by Micheal Massi and the stewards. It also set the bar for how competitive this season was going to be between Mercedes and Red Bull Racing, but even more so between Hamilton and Verstappen.

The next race on the calendar was the Emilia Romagna GP. To Lewis and Mercedes it seemed the like there was a sense of the inevitable about the season ahead: the Briton was surely on course for an eighth world title. Unfortunately though, before the end of the weekend that feeling would completely disappear. Verstappen, starting in third, made a

RACE TO 2021 DRIVER CHAMPION

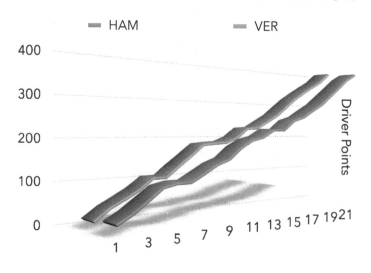

"*Super Max*" start. Hamilton, starting from pole, saw Verstappen not only overtake his team mate Perez but fly past the number 44 as well. With Max leading the race after lap 1, we saw something that we rarely ever see Hamilton do. He made a mistake. Hamilton flew off the track halfway through the race, which could have meant a huge point loss for him if it wasn't for the red flag, which allowed him to change his front wing and tires to race back to second place (from 9th). While his drive from 9th to 2nd place showed an absolute superb drive, it was the mistake that caused him to go back to 9th that showed that Hamilton was indeed for the first time in a long long time under pressure from another driver.

The next couple of races saw Max and Lewis swing back and forth in the Driver Championship lead, with Red Bull dominating in Monaco, Austria, Azerbaijan and France while Mercedes was dominant in Portugal and Spain. The next season-changing event happened in the home race of Lewis Hamilton at Silverstone. The British GP would be the first race of the season to introduce a sprint-race format (worth 3 points), which was a quick no pitstop race of 100km on Saturday. During this sprint race the racing style of Max Verstappen to hold Lewis Hamilton behind him was considered fierce at the very least. It was Max who won the sprint race and started the Grand Prix on pole position. Through board radios and the interviews after the sprint race, Hamilton showed his annoyance at the racing style of Max Verstappen and that hinted at the fact that he would no longer back off if Max were to make a forceful move on the track. Not even 24 hours later, we would see exactly this happening in the "Copse Crash". After a rumble and a tumble in the opening lap between Verstappen and Hamilton, the two drivers were heading into Copse Corner almost side by side at 290 km per hour. Lewis' left front tire clipped the car of Max which caused the Dutchman to fly off track and into the barriers at an extremely high impact. Hamilton was awarded a 5 second penalty for causing the crash but thanks to superb drive he managed to fight his way back from 4th to 1st after serving his penalty. This would be the start of the fierce racing between the two title contenders. To add fuel to the fire, Bottas in a horrific first lap crashed against both the Red Bulls one race later in Hungary. While Hamilton nor Mercedes cannot be blamed by the mistake of Bottas, this meant that in the span of two races and two crashes, Hamilton had regained the lead to the championship.

Lady Luck then decided to fortune team Red Bull as F1 returned from the summer break. A rained-out Spa track in Belgium meant that Verstappen would win the race simply by getting pole position and driving 2 laps behind a safety car, while Hamilton was driving in third. After Max Verstappen was his home race in The Netherlands, he had regained the lead in the championship and felt the momentum switch back to him until a disastrous pitstop in Monza, Italy. Max was leading the race in Monza until a he had a slow pitstop that took more than 8 seconds, causing Hamilton to catch up to Max. This meant the two drivers were once again side by side. As they headed into turn 1 of the Italian Grand Prix, Max, who was behind Lewis as they went into the corner, did drove Lewis into the gravel and ended the race for both of them. This time, it was Verstappen who had caused the incident and was hence awarded a 5 place-grid penalty for the next race in Russia. Now you might be wondering, how did Max get a 5 place grid penalty while Lewis only got a 5 second penalty? The reason for this is is because Lewis was not out of the race in the British GP and could therefore be awarded a penalty in the race, while Max was already classified as a DNF (**Did Not Finish**) and could not be awarded a penalty for the Italian GP. The only action the stewards could take would be a grid penalty or a fine. Since the stewards did not want to encourage racing to the point of crashing, they felt like they had to give a grid penalty to set precedent for the rest of the season. While racing didn't get less fierce, this would be the last collision between Max and Lewis of the season. The next races would all be tense battles that led to the championship still being undecided by the time we got the to second last race of the season; The Saudi Arabia Grand Prix. With qualifying already ending in drama as Max Verstappen hit the barriers in the final corner on a lap that was likely to set him in pole position, we started the race with Lewis in first and Max in third place. After the first couple of laps, it was Lewis in first place and Max in second place as Schumacher hit the wall and caused, at first, a virtual safety car. This caused Hamilton to pit as it would save him time during the safety car. However, Verstappen decided to stay out putting him in the lead of the race. A lap later, the red flag was announced. This race then became a race that would go down in history as one of the most complicated races of all times. At the race restart, Max was able to change his tires (as Lewis did in Italy in the second race of the season) meaning both teams had completed their mandatory pit stops. This will be discussed more in the rules chapter, but each driver must make one pitstop where they switch between tire compounds (e.g. from soft to medium tires). This was an advantageous result for Verstappen as he therefore overtook Hamilton during the safety car and red flag and were now both on the same tires. However, at the first corner of the restarted race Hamilton had a superb start and would have overtaken Verstappen if Verstappen didn't force him off track. Not even 2 turns later, the race returned to Red Flag as several cars had crashed. During this Red Flag, negotiations took place on the punishment for Verstappen, miscommunications and many radio messages were sent that confused everyone and almost no rules could be looked at to help the fans understand what was happening. The result was that Hamilton would restart from pole place with Ocon and Verstappen behind him. This time, it was Verstappen with the superb start and he was able to overtake both Ocon and Hamilton to get his first place back. However, after Verstappen again was found to be too aggressive during the race, he was told to hand back a position to Hamilton. Unfortunately, Hamilton had not been told about the fact that Verstappen had to give back the spot, and when Verstappen slowed down to give the spot back Hamilton didn't expect this. The two cars had a minor collision but were both able to race until the finish. The confusion and the amount of interference in the race by the FIA and stewards was probably the most discussed talking point as we went into the final race of the season with both drivers tied in points. The Saudi Arabia Grand Prix and everything that happened throughout the race was absolutely a consideration for the stewards on how they would act during the final race of the season and why the final race concluded in the way it did. After criticism from both teams after the Saudi Arabia GP the stewards had all agreed to let teams race as much as possible without interfering if it wasn't absolutely necessary. This meant that we went into the Abu Dhabi GP with Max Verstappen on Pole and Lewis Hamilton right behind him. Thanks to a superb start by Hamilton, he was leading the race after turn 1 and was side by side with Max Verstappen at turn 6 where he felt there wasn't enough room on the track so he had to take evasive action and cut two corners. The stewards decided no actions were necessary, consistent to how they said they were going to monitor this race. From here on out, it was clear that Mercedes had the upper hand as Hamilton cruised away into a huge lead from Verstappen,. After Hamilton had to pit for new tired, Red Bull decided to keep Perez out on track on old tires in order to slow Hamilton down. Sergio Perez did such a fantastic job holding up the Mercedes that it is estimated that Hamilton lost over 20 seconds in 2 laps. This allowed Max to temporarily catch up to Hamilton and close any pit-window, which becomes a critical point at the end of the race. Hamilton remained in the lead until there were only 8 laps remaining. Nicholas Latifi, had crashed into the barriers and caused a safety car. With only one lap remaining, and again some confusing messages from the FIA and stewards on how the race would resume, Max Verstappen was racing right behind Lewis Hamilton. Thanks to a strategic Red Bull call, Verstappen was on fresh new Soft Tires while Hamilton was on old Hard Tires. Hamilton could not bet to switch tires as Perez had closed the gap between Verstappen and Hamilton, which means that Hamilton would have lost track position if he would have switched tires. The finale of the season couldn't have been scripted better in a movie, Verstappen overtook Hamilton with only half a lap to go and become the first Dutch Formula 1 Champion. While the controversy of how the rules should be applied was forgotten as the newly crowned champion celebrated, it wasn't forgotten the next couple of days.

Even after the season ended in December the drama continued. In the days following the controversy of Abu Dhabi there are a couple of things all teams need to do. The first is the post-season tire test. Since Pirelli is introducing a whole new set of tires, this one is quite crucial for the teams to prepare their 2022 car as best as possible. After the test days, the next event is a photoshoot of all the cars that participated this season. All cars appeared with the exception of one team: Mercedes. They were still too upset with how the final laps of the 2021 season went down and refused to display their car for the photoshoot. This meant that, one day later, at the Award Ceremony of Formula 1 in Monaco, the Mercedes' car would not have an image to display, even though they were the winners of the constructor's championship. To add fuel to the fire, Toto Wolff and Lewis Hamilton did not show up at the award ceremony at all. Again, Lewis was key to this event as he got the 2nd place trophy for this season. His teammate, however, Valteri Bottas did attend. The rules state that it is mandatory for all teams and all drivers to attend to this event. While Mercedes initially protested the win of Max Verstappen they did not appeal the decision of the FIA to disregard the protest. How the drama and controversy of the last race will affect the 2022 season is still very much unclear. Will there be a penalty for Lewis Hamilton and Mercedes for not showing at the photoshoot nor the award ceremony?

FERRARI VS MCLAREN

	Ferrari	McLaren
Championship result:	3rd	4th
Best race result:	2nd	1st
Wins:	0	1
Pole positions:	2	1
Points:	323.5	275
DNFs:	2	2

Two giants fighting to restore their old glory. Up until 2019, Ferrari was fighting with Mercedes and Red Bull for the title almost every year but then something strange happened. Ferrari was accused of having breached some regulations regarding their engine and suffered in straight line speed the following seasons as they adjusted their engine to meet all of the new regulations set by the FIA for Ferrari. McLaren has been trying to find its way back to the glory days since they started using Honda Engines in the hybrid era. They had switched to Renault engines in 2018 and this season chose the most powerful engine of Mercedes to fight with the top teams. The two teams in pre-season seemed to be head to head with McLaren just edging out Ferrari as we saw the season kick off in Bahrain. It was Lando Norris who shone in the first half of the season as he was out qualifying and out racing not only both Ferraris but also his teammate, Daniel Ricciardo. It was mainly due to Lando that McLaren was edging out Ferrari consistently throughout the first half of the season as McLaren had been in third place in the constructor championship until Race 13! Something they have not been able to achieve in a long time. However, Ferrari was also busy with their own successes. Carlos Sainz who had just joined the team was matching the incredible performance of Charles Leclerc in Sainz' very first season. Normally, as we saw with Daniel Ricciardo, drivers need at least a season to get used to the the team and the general drive and feel of the car on all the different tracks. While McLaren was leading the constructor championship throughout the first half of the season, this could have been a different story if things in Monaco had gone slightly different for Ferrari. In his hometown nonetheless, Charles Leclerc took an extraordinary pole position. It was a complete surprise to almost everybody that a Ferrari would out qualify not only Red Bull but also Mercedes. The surprises continued when on the final lap of qualifying, that very same Ferrari was crashed into the oh so dangerous turn at the swimming pool. This crash would later cause Leclerc not to race in Monaco, meaning the pole was lost and only one out of two cars competed. Carlos Sainz did end up getting 2nd place but with Lando Norris in 3rd place the team only gained 3 points on McLaren.

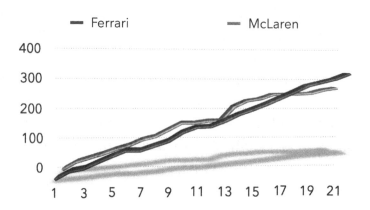

As the season continued, both teams were not only scoring consistently but they were scoring very high points. In fact in the first half of the season all top 5 finishes featured either a McLaren or a Ferrari, but the majority of them saw both. During the British GP we saw Leclerc achieve a masterful 2nd place and even fight with Hamilton to try and retain 1st place in the race. What seemed like a real turning point in the season was the Italian GP. As you may recall, Hamilton and Verstappen had crashed each other out of the race, and suddenly there was an opportunity for other teams to try and win the race. It only took a couple of laps for both Daniel Ricciardo (P1) and Lando Norris (P2) to see themselves leading the race and securing the only 1,2 finish of the entire season. It seemed like this had given McLaren a huge amount of momentum as they went into the next race in Russia. It was Lando Norris instead of Daniel Ricciardo this time that was leading the race with only a few laps to go. The race would have been surely won by McLaren if it wasn't for the sudden change in weather. The weather drastically changed as clouds started rolling over the track and teams had to decide what to do with their strategies. McLaren along with most of the other teams thought the best strategy was to switch to inter (rain) tires, which would mean Norris making a pitstop and potentially losing first place to Hamilton if Hamilton choice not to do the same. However, Norris decided to stay out and try and drive in the wet on slick tires, which seemed like a good call based on the rain forecast as the rain was very light. The rain started to completely pour down and within a couple of corners Norris found himself off-track and sliding to the pit-lane for wet tires. With the mess on track due to everyone pitting at different times, the best performing drive out of McLaren and Ferrari was suddenly Carlos Sainz. Luckily the combined score of Daniel Ricciardo and Lando Norris was enough to extend their lead from Ferrari, but this would be the last time this season that they would be able to do so.

Throughout the final races of the season, Ferrari put down the same phenomenal performance they had been showing at the beginning of the season but it seemed like McLaren had to shift their development focus to the 2022 car and couldn't continue to develop their 2021 season car. This meant that McLaren was only able to score 21 points in the final 5 races of the season while Ferrari scored 73 points. While the battle didn't end in the fierce way that the season started, we can absolutely expect these two to be looking up rather than down the packing order. Ferrari achieving a third place in the championship again and nearly getting 200 points more than they did in 2020, is a huge accomplishment and is a sign of things to come for next season.

ALPHA TAURI VS ALPINE

	Alpha Tauri	Alpine
Championship result:	6th	5th
Best race result:	3rd	1st
Wins:	0	1
Pole positions:	0	0
Points:	142	155
DNFs:	7	5

In a similar fashion to Ferrari and McLaren, we saw another battle unfold on the track this year between teams that both showed a surprise performance. Alpine, formally known as Renault, has been trying to fight its way up to the top of the grid but hasn't been as successful as was hoped. This year, they had changed their name to Alpine (their sports-car brand) and signed former F1 World Champion Fernando Alonso. The team's goal for the season was to be fighting with the top three, and while they were no able to do so there were several signs of improvements that look promising for the future of Alpine. First, a huge problem that the Renault engines had in the past was their reliability. This season Alpine only had 5 DNF's and only 2 of those were due to problems with their engine units. Beyond this, the power of the Renault engine seems to have significantly increased as the Alpines were often in the top 10 when it came to Top Speed. This shows that if Alpine is able to make a more competitive chassis next year, they should be better able to compete. Their biggest competitors this year were Alpha

Tauri, a team previously known as Toro Rosso, or Red Bull's sister team. While the team is commonly known as Red Bull's secondary team, for their more junior drivers, this year the team was not just a fun junior team. Pierre Gasly was able to qualify in the top 6 cars 9 times this season. No other team besides McLaren, Red Bull and Mercedes were able to beat that number. However, when it came to race pace and finishing results, Alpha Tauri often struggled. Whether this was due to their drivers being less capable of saving the tires or whether that is because the car just didn't have the race pace is unclear. However, the high qualifying performance meant by race 10 (almost halfway through the season) Alpha Tauri was in 5th place in the constructor championship. The second half of the season saw Alpine excel, with Ocon winning a race and Alonso getting second place. The combination of the two drivers meant that by the end of the season Alpine would conquer 5th place and Alpha Tauri would have to settle in 6th. However, one big achievement that the team walked away with this season is the fact that

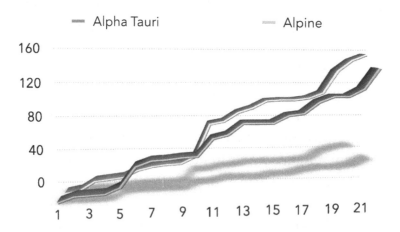

Pierre Gasly finished the season in 9th place and had 110 point to his name, only 5 less than Daniel Ricciardo. Neither Alonso nor Ocon came close to the point tally set by Pierre Gasly, even though Gasly didn't win a single race. I think we're yet to see the full capabilities of Gasly, and next season should prove to be another good one for him.

CHAPTER 2

RULES AND REGULATIONS

Before exploring the new rules and regulations lets cover some basics first

A big part of the 2022 season are the new regulations that are coming into play next season. However, let's first start with some of the basics before we get into the new rules and what they will mean. A standard Formula 1 weekend consists of three days but how these three days look like depends on the race format that is being held each weekend. Throughout the 2021 season we saw three weekends using a Sprint Race Format but these sprint races will return in a different format in 2022. Hence, we will not cover these exceptional race formats in this chapter but instead we will focus on how a classic race weekend looks like and what rules are applied to on each day of the weekend.

THURSDAY

The weekend officially starts on Thursday[1] with drivers and team interviews. Some teams also do a traditional track walk. It is mandatory, unless the driver has asked for an exception, to attend the press conference for each driver during a slot of 45 minutes on this day.

Before the start of the weekend each driver also has to make a tire selection for the entire weekend. Each weekend there are 5 tires, Soft, Medium, Hard, Inter- and Full Wets. Teams do not have to choose their rain tires (which are Inter and Full Wet tires), but each driver does have to pick 10 sets off slick (dry) tires for the entire weekend. Choosing your tire split correctly before the weekend can be a first step to winning a race for a driver. Most weekends teams tend to choose around 4-6 sets of soft tires 2-4 sets of medium tires and 2-4 sets of hard tires. Once you have used a set in practice or qualifying, the tires will be worn and will perform worse if used during a race.

FRIDAY

On Friday there is Free Practice (FP) 1 and 2, which each team can use to optimise their car set up. Since These Free Practices have been in place since 2006 and are used by teams to find the optimal set up of the car before Qualifying

---

[1] With the exception of the Monaco GP- this GP starts on Wednesday, FP1 and FP2 are held on Thursday, Friday is a rest day, and the rest of the weekend remains the same.

on Saturday. Besides some small rules for tire changes in FP 1 and 2, there are no major rules in this part of the weekend except for that cars cannot block each other and pit-lane safety needs to be adhered to. Teams do not have to use the same engine in Free Practice as in the race. Hence, you can sometimes think a team like Alpha Tauri looks super strong in practice but this can change in the race. At the end of each FP, drivers can also line up at the starting line or pit-lane exit (this depends on the track) to practice a practice start. Each Free Practice lasts 60 minutes and cars can use any and all components on Friday, without any obligations to use these in Qualifying or in the race.

SATURDAY

Before we get into the slightly more complex rules that must be adhered to on Saturday, or Qualifying Day, it is important to understand a couple of things regarding the engines used in Formula 1. In 2014, Formula 1 entered an era called the Hybrid Era, which meant the switch from V8 to V6 Hybrid engines. The main reason for switching from V8 engines to V6 engines was to be more environmentally friendly as a sport by reducing the engines and introducing the hybrid components. The introduction of hybrid engines meant that engines have several modes available that can be used depending on the scenario. A standard race mode will allow adequate harvesting to keep the battery supplied with energy that can be deployed through the lap – without draining the battery fully and thereby compromising the following lap. It will also typically run lower maximum revs than the qualifying mode and a setting of ignition timing that keeps the valves and piston crowns at a safer temperature. You can imagine that running an engine at its maximum capacity can be extremely useful when you are doing qualifying lap, but is dangerous to do for 72 laps when you are in a race. You can compare this to sports like Track and Field (athletics) where an athlete may choose to save energy in the first 70 laps of a race and sprint home the final 2. Typically there are several – up to nine – modes in between the two extremes. These modes are crucial for teams to think about as they determine not only the engine life, but also reliability and fuel consumption.

Saturday is when we have some more serious rules and regulations. During FP3 the drivers usually gear up for qualifying and the teams try to find that ideal setup to set a blistering quick qualifying time. Between FP3 and Qualifying no changes can be made to the car, except for repairs. Hence, it's critical that teams try and get the car perfect before they start their qualifying lap.

After FP3 the first major moment of the weekend comes in the form of qualifying. Qualifying consists of three knock out stages(Q1, Q2, Q3) which lasts 18 minutes, 15 minutes and 12 minutes respectively. In Q1 the five slowest cars are eliminated, in Q2 the next 5 slowest cars are eliminated and in Q3 the top 10 starting order is determined. Cars that take the chequered flag at the end of Q3 will return to parc fermé for scrutineering, rather than to their garage. This is always a scary moment for the teams because during scrutineering the cars are simply turned off like a road car, rather than slowly cooled and controlled switching off. Hence, three engineers from the team are allowed to join this process to make sure the car gets shut down properly (adding cooling fans, etc). As soon as the car is shutdown, it will be checked thoroughly for legality for the race. The FIA can also choose to do random checks and will select at least six cars for in-depth checks at the end of practice.

© Getty Images

The hours after qualifying can be chaotic as all the cars are moving from and to their garages and scrutineering checks. If you like working under pressure, this is the time you want to be on an F1 crew because you have only a three and a half hours to work with a car that has been pushed to its limit in the qualifying session. In only a few hours the car needs to be inspected, prepared for the race, and possibly even be repaired. After the three and a half hours are over we enter a period referred to as Parc Fermé.

Parc Fermé is a beautiful French phrase used in a lot of motor sports, which in very simple terms just means that your car can only undergo very few changes in this period. Overnight, the car literally has to be sealed, which some teams do by throwing a wrapping around the car. There are 22 subclauses that cover what is allowed to be changed during this period so here they are summarised in 11 quick bullet points. (These are simplified of course, the actual rules have a lot of technical details included)

ALLOWED DURING PARC FERMÉ:

Teams are **only** allowed to:

1. Teams are allowed to start engines;
2. Add or remove fuel and fit a fuel breather
3. Remove wheels
4. Take out the spark plugs to better inspect the engine
5. Fit the cooling fans or fit heaters
6. Fit a jump battery to access and test electronic systems
7. Bled brakes and drain engine oil
8. Adjust the front wing angle
9. Adjust wing mirrors, pedals and seat belts
10. Fill up the driver's drink bottle
11. Repair of genuine accident damage (under the watch of an assigned scrutineer)

SUNDAY

Sunday in Formula 1 is race day! The most important day of the weekend, as this is the day that teams can score the points that determine their standings in the championship. Before the race, we are in Parc Fermé which means the same rules as Saturday apply. About half an hour before the race begins, all the starting cars can do 1 or 2 out-laps to get their cars to the starting grid. If any car gets some small damages during these laps, the engineers can try and fix the car on-track until the start of the race. Then, two minutes prior to the start of the race the cars can do one more lap around the track called the "Formation Lap", to make sure all engines are turned on and working correctly before lining up to the lights to start the race. During the formation lap, the cars can drive at any pace but cannot over take one another, meaning that the pole position determines the maximum pace for the rest of the grid. The starting light sequence of the race will only commence once the final car is in its correct starting spot. At this point, the 5 starting lights will turn on, one at a time, until they are all turned off at the same time. This is the start of the race.

During the race there are a lot of rules and sanctions that can follow a rule break, probably too many to mention and impossible if I want to keep this book under 1,000 pages. Hence the most common ones are mentioned here:

- Jumping the start
- Causing an unnecessary collision
- Corner cutting
- Passing under caution
- Speeding in the pit lane
- Blocking another driver as he attempts to pass

There are many different punishments for breaking the rules of Formula 1. Finally, in some races you will see a term called track limits which describes certain part of the tracks where the drivers must stay on track with at least 2 wheels. These track limits are usually white lines These three are the most common:

- **Drive-Through Penalty**: A driver must drive through the pit lane within three laps.
- **Time Penalty:** A driver gets a 5, 10 or 15 second penalty. That means at the next pitstop the car has to be fully stopped for this amount of time. If there are no pitstops left, this time will be deducted from the finishing time.
- **Grid Penalty** : A driver gets a penalty that contains the number of spots he drops in the grid. If this is during the race he will have to give back some positions, if this is before or after a race this will happen at the starting grid of the first upcoming race.

Upon finishing the race points get handed out to the top 10 drivers.
- 1st Place: 25 points
- 2nd Place: 18 points

- 3rd Place: 15 points
- 4th Place: 12 points
- 5th Place: 10 points
- 6th Place: 8 points
- 7th Place: 6 points
- 8th Place: 4 points
- 9th Place: 2 points
- 10th Place: 1 point

If the leader has completed more than two laps but less than 75% of the original race distance, the above shown points will be halved. If less than two laps are driven, no points will be awarded, and if more than 75% of original race distance is driven full points will be awarded. If drivers finish tied on points the positions get decided on results (first most wins, then most 2nd places, etc). Any driver can change teams during the season. In this case, his points with the previous team get added to his Drivers' points tally. But, the Constructors' points tally goes to the respective teams. We've seen this happen when Alex Albon took over for Pierre Gasly in Red Bull in 2018.

POST-RACE PARC FERMÉ

At the end of the weekend, after the race has finished and most viewers are tuned out, the cars that finish the race must again go into Parc Fermé. At this point they will get checked by the scrutineers again and until everything has been properly checked the stewards can still decided to change any finishing classification. In 2021, the FIA added a rule that after every race one car at random will get checked and may stay under Parc Fermé until much later in the evening for more detailed checks. This sums up the rules and regulations that we saw in the 2021 season.

We are entering a new era of rules and regulations of formula 1.

If you're not very interested in the technical rules and regulations of Formula 1 then you can just read the next part and then move onto one of the next chapters to read more about what is happening next season.

(Formula1.com, 2021)

Every now and then Formula 1 make sure that the competition stays interesting between teams by introducing completely new regulations every decade or so, which the teams have to agree on. We have been in the hybrid era since 2014 which has been dominated by Mercedes predominantly and will end as of 2021. We are now entering a new era which will continue to make use of the hybrid engine as we know it, however there is a lot of rules and regulations coming up that are going to make the competition even more interesting. The first very interesting rule that we will see in the 2022 season of Formula 1 is the budget.[2]

As of this season, we will have a budget cap for each team that will limit the spending. This means that the smaller teams have more of a chance to compete against the larger teams since the differences in spending will be reduced by the budget cap. In the past the top three teams which are Ferrari, Mercedes and Red Bull have had a lot more resources that they could apply to make their car the best performing car. The budget cap is set at $145 million. To put this in perspective, this is far beyond what Haas spends every year but is about what a medium-sized team like Alpine would spend. The top teams like Red Bull, Mercedes and Ferarri will have to cut their budgets by about $100 to $200 million. Resources are not directly in correlation with the performance of a team however it is likely that a team that has higher resources has a higher R&D department and therefore is more likely to develop their car better than their competitors. One thing that is important to mention for this budget cap is that the salary of the drivers are not included. Hence, the bigger teams are still more likely to be able to

2 Formula 1, 2021

snatch the better drivers as they can pay more salary to the drivers.

Next, let's take a look at the tires. These are looking completely different to anything we've seen in the last seven years with thinner rubber tires but bigger tires overall. Tires are a huge component of a car, not only in terms of team strategies but also in terms of aerodynamics and cooling. This means that if a car was working perfectly in the 2021 season it might be working very poorly in 2022 due to the new tires. On a larger Formula 1 scale this means that all teams had to completely redesign their cars for 2022, and this is a very time-consuming and costly procedure. Teams like Haas decided to focus on the design of the 2022 car a year in advance already and therefore were dead last in 2021. Other teams like Red Bull and Mercedes were very focused on winning the 2021 season and only could spare a couple of resources throughout the season to focus on 2022.

Besides the tires and the budget, the whole design of a Formula 1 car has also been changed. The new 2022 designs that all team must follow are created to improve overtaking and driving behind other cars. In the last era, cars that were following other cars experienced a phenomenon called Dirty Air which means that because of the complex designs of the car in front of them, air was coming from all sort of angles at their car which meant a reduction in downforce and increase in overheating of the tires. Since the 2022 cars will be a completely different design, which brings all competitors closer together. It's always going to be a guess if a team has figured out a really fast design or not. Teams cannot really copy each other as the first test in Barcelona is far too close to the start of the season for teams to try and replicate one another. Talking about the Barcelona Test that took place in the last week of February 2022, we saw a huge amount of different designs on cars. Red Bull had a side-pod that was called intriguing by all the other teams and will even be checked by the FIA for legality. McLaren and Ferrari each took a very different design approach to Red Bull and Mercedes, but all four teams look fast. The only team that didn't look very successful during the first batch of pre-season testing? Haas, the only team who invested all of its efforts into designing their 2022 car. We'll go more into this in the next chapter.

So we've covered the tires and the car but what about the engine? Well, the engine actually did not change much because the FIA, together with all teams, enforced an engine freeze between 2021 and 2022 due to Honda dropping out of Formula 1 and Red Bull Technologies entering F1. However, while officially Honda has left F1, there are still four cars in 2022 that have the Honda Racing Corporation (HRC) logos in their cars. Red Bull even admitted that "Honda is still involved with their people and we have almost the same people as last year". So the engine freeze seems like a smart play from Red Bull Racing to keep the competition between their Honda Engine and Mercedes' own engine the same as previous season in order to maximise the chassis influence on performance.

There is one more important change that should be mentioned if you want to be fully aware of all the differences in 2022 and that is the change on how the Sprint Weekends will be held. The Spring Weekend was introduced in 2021 and we saw three of these weekend in England, Italy and Brazil. Last year, the weekend was split up between Free Practice 1 and Qualifying on Friday, Free Practice 2 and Sprint Race on Saturday and the Race on Sunday. Qualifying on Friday happened like how qualifying would happen on a normal weekend, with the exception that all cars needed to qualify on the Red (Soft) Tires. On Saturday, drivers had to race a 25% length of the race on Sunday and the top three drivers could earn 3, 2 or 1 points respectively. On Sunday the race would continue from the finishing order of Saturday's race and would take place as usual.

This year, there are two main changes for the 2022 sprints. The first change is more of term change than anything else and won't have any impact on the championship. The qualifying on Friday determines the "Pole Position winner", which is a price handed out by Pirelli for the car that is the fastest in qualifying. Last year, this title would go to the winner of the sprint race on Saturday. The change in this title doesn't actually change anything in the qualifying rules. The bigger change this year is that instead of the top 3, the top 8 drivers on Saturday's sprint race will now earn points. The point system will still be the same with the driver who finishes P1 receiving eight points, down to one point for the driver in P8.

CHAPTER 3

EVERYTHING YOU NEED TO KNOW FOR SEASON 2022

Team Haas in Financial and Driver trouble

On the 24th of February 2022 , when Russia invaded Ukraine, a lot of sporting communities reacted quickly to ban any Russian presence in the World Cup, Paralympics (because Putin waited until the end of the Olympics to invade) and also the FIA decided to not allow Russian presence. Haas, being in a title sponsor relationship with Uralkali, a Russian fertiliser, was put in a very difficult spot as Uralkali is not only a Russian company but one that has close relationships with the Russian State and Putin. After 7 days of war and Uralkali's presence with the Russian State not wavering, Haas had decided to break the sponsorship deal with Uralkali. As Haas is a very small team with limited finances, it is yet to see if Haas has the funds to survive as a standalone team throughout this season. If the Haas financial problems become detrimental there are only three options left for Haas this season. The best scenario is that Haas finds another title sponsor that is willing to invest significant money into the team. The other two scenarios are lot more gloomy with Haas either being bought up by an existing Formula 1 team as a daughter / sister team (e.g. RedBull/AlphaTauri) or being bought up by a non-existing team. The final option would be declaring bankruptcy and exiting Formula 1 all together. If Haas can survive it's monetary problems they still have one more problem as their title partnership sponsor also included one of their two drivers: Nikita Mazepin. While Mazepin was probably the worst driver on the grid, he did bring in a huge amount of money, marketing and engineering capabilities. Now that Mazepin has been confirmed not to be part of the team, Haas has replaced Mazepin with Kevin Magnussen, who had been with Haas for multiple years before being kicked out of the team to be replaced by Mazepin. The results that Magnussen will put on the board will most likely be far better than Mazepin, but will he perform well enough to keep crashes and extra unnecessary costs to a minimum?

Who looked strong during Pre-Season Testing?

Pre-Season testing is about as difficult to interpret as interpreting the price of an NFT these days. However, while it is hard to interpret, we can still take some key takeaways from the double testing week we saw this year. Let's start with reliability. From a reliability perspective, all teams are fairing quite well if we compare it to some previous years. However, we have a couple of teams that have struggled more than others; Haas, McLaren, Alpha Romeo are the three teams that have had most problems. If these teams are not able to address the problems before the season starts, they could lose a lot of points by not finishing races (DNF).

Next to reliability the trust and feel in the car is extremely important and drivers were very vocal about how they felt about their cars this year. A word that got used more often than any other word was *"porpoising"* . Porpoising describes the uncontrollable bouncing off the car, which can happen due to a cycle of aerodynamic unloading and reloading of the car, as these cars are designed to suck the car towards the floor. Even during the final stages of pre-season testing, Mercedes and McLaren were struggling to keep this under control. However, porpoising wasn't the only problem that teams experienced. General control and drivability of the car is also something extremely important as drivers must be able to predict exactly what their car plans to do when they are driving at the maximum speed. Mercedes, surprisingly, also wasn't too happy with this as their car was deemed unpredictable. The same feeling applied to Alpine and Aston Martin in the first week, but as we got to the second week of pre-season testing, this feeling changed for these two teams.

Finally, let's talk about performance. Who set the fastest times of pre-season testing and who do the drivers think are going to be the team to beat this year? Well, it was at the very end of the two weeks of pre-season testing that the fastest time was set on track. The current World Champion, Max Verstappen, set a time that was more than half a second faster than any other team was able to do throughout the two weeks. In an interview, he also warned this was not yet the top speed of the Red Bull. After Red Bull, it was Ferrari who set the fastest time on track with Mercedes, Alpine and Alpha Romeo following closely. The drivers meanwhile believe it is going to be Ferrari that will start to set that pace in the first couple of races, and while it would be amazing to see the prancing horses back in form, we still don't know if any team has been sandbagging and hiding their true performance. Mercedes, as the current constructors champion, is a team that should not be underestimated as they have hidden their full performance in other seasons too. If I were to predict right now I would say the title fight is most likely to be between Ferrari, Mercedes and Red Bull, while the battle for best of the rest will be between Alpine, Aston Martin and Alpha Tauri.

Max Verstappen will want to prove he is a worthy Champion.

Max Verstappen will be driving with the number 1 on his car this year as he gets to use this number being the current Formula 1 World Champion. Since Michael Massi has been removed from his position after what happened in Abu Dhabi, Mercedes and Lewis Hamilton may feel like they were proven right that max won under wrong circumstances. Max will very much like to prove Mercedes wrong by winning the title again this year. Sebastian Vettel has warned Lewis Hamilton that he expects Max Verstappen to flourish as

Formula 1's defending world champion. Meanwhile, Hamilton is still looking to break the record for all-time most won Formula 1 World Champions, as he hopes to secure his 8th title. He is currently tied with Michael Schumacher and he believes he is as 'dangerous' a driver as he has ever been. At the same time, if Ferrari have a car that can compete with Red Bull and Mercedes, Charles Leclerc will want to prove himself as the world champion driver that Ferrari believe him to be. This could be the first year that he can prove that he has what Vettel did not have at Ferrari.

Albon & Magnussen looking for comeback and Zhou looking to prove himself.

We've got a great new driver lineup this year with not one, not two but three driver changes. First, we have Kevin Magnussen. Magnussen has returned from a year out of Formula 1 and said he wasn't expecting to ever be back in the sport. He has scored 158 points in Formula 1 already in 118 race starts. That absolutely makes him one of the more senior drivers in the sport and he should look to prove to Haas that he has still got it. He'll know how fragile his F1 seat is and therefore going to be trying to convince Haas and everyone watching that he is the driver that should remain in the team. Next, we've got our only Chinese driver- Guanyu Zhou. While we have seen a lot of other drivers enter F1 through the F2 path, like Lando Norris, George Russel, Mick Schumacher and

Alex Albon, it will be interesting to see how Guanyu Zhou makes the switch to the sport. He has had some good performances in Asia but last season the young driver only came third in Formula 2, in what was not a highly competitive season (Oscar Piastri won F2 but did not get an F1 seat). With Zhou joining Alpha Romeo, he has a golden opportunity to show his worth against ex-mercedes driver Bottas. If he can beat Bottas in his first season he will have proven a fantastic driver on the grid. Finally, our third new driver this season is Alex Albon. The Thai Driver has had a very interesting career having joined Toro Rosso after coming 2nd in Formula 2 and moving to Red Bull after only 6 months in the sport as he replaced Pierre Gasly at Red Bull. However, his Formula 1 journey came to an end after a season and a half at Red Bull as Checo Perez took his seat. Now, after a year of not being in formula 1, he gets to prove himself again at Williams where he will be racing against Nicholas Latifi. Latifi was almost always out qualified and beaten by his former teammate George Russel, and if Albon thinks he's a great driver, he should be able to do the same. It will be interesting to see what happens here!

CHAPTER 4

YOUR SEASON 2022 QUESTIONS ANSWERED

Every question you ever asked answered in less then 10 minutes of reading - Let's go!

HONDA IS LEAVING FORMULA 1- HOW WILL RED BULL'S ENGINE PERFORM NEXT SEASON?

This might be surprising but this question can be answered with quite a bit of confidence. The answer is: Red Bull's Engine will probably be exactly as competitive as Honda's engine. The reason for this is because the 2022 season has agreed on and power unit development freeze. In February 2021, all teams gave unanimous approval at a meeting of the Formula 1 Commission, with the FIA, Formula 1, the teams and the power unit manufacturers to freeze engine development until 2023. Since Red Bull acquired the Honda Engine technology, this means that they can keep their development and all other teams will remain equal in their development. Most likely Honda will remain slightly slower than the Mercedes engine but will be competitive enough to compete if Red Bull have a good chassis.

WHAT IS ALLOWED AND WHAT IS NOT ALLOWED DURING YELLOW AND RED FLAGS?

We're seeing more and more safety measures in Formula 1. We've seen the halo get added to F1 cars and we're also seeing more and more safety flags. A yellow flag just means there is danger (like a car has stopped near the track or in a slow part of the track), double yellow flag means there is more danger. Under the double yellow flag, qualifying lap times will not count in order to incentivise drivers not to continue full speed driving during double yellow flags. Finally when things get really dangerous the race director can trigger a Virtual Safety car (VSC) which slows everybody down to 40% of their race speed. The next most dangerous thing after a VSC is an actual safety car. This means they send out an actual safety car where everybody has to stay behind it until the safety car ends. At this point the lapped cars unlap themselves (with the exception of Abu Dhabi '21) and then the race is restarted by the leader.

During Safety Cars and Virtual Safety cars it can be very appealing for teams to go into the pitstop as the other drivers that are driving on track are not driving at full speed. This means that in comparison to a non-safety car situation, cars lose less of their lead. This is a piece of strategy that is a bit of luck, but certain tracks are more likely to see a safety car than others, so using those statistics to determine your strategy can be very useful for teams. Azerbaijan (Baku), Singapore and Brazil (São Paulo) are the top three tracks in the 2022 season that have the most likelihood of seeing a safety car, so most teams will wait with their pitstop until a safety car takes place.

Beyond yellow flags we also sometimes see a red flag. Red flags are the most severe measure the race control can take when something happens on track, as a red flag temporary stops the race. During the red flag teams are allowed to change their tires (yes, this would satisfy the 1 pitstop per race rule) and even conduct repairs on their tires. This is a huge rule because this means if a driver has not pitted yet when a red flag is shown, that driver will gain a huge advantage over anyone who has already pitted. The 'red flag repair' rule was introduced to enable cars to get ready for changed weather conditions, imagine if it went from super sunny in qualifying to extreme rain during a race, but in the last couple of years red flags have become more common as safety has become more important.

CAN FORMULA 1 DRIVERS PEE DURING THE RACE?

Yes, but this means peeing in their suits - so most drivers choose not to.

HOW MANY RACES WILL THERE BE IN 2022?

Provided Covid-19 doesn't change the schedule, there will be 22 races in 2022. This means we will almost have a race every weekend while the season is on! After pre-season in Barcelona and Bahrain, the season will start with the first race in Bahrain. The season that progresses to Sandi Arabia and Australia and will then continue in Europe through the European Summer. After Europe, Formula 1 moves on to Asia, North America and we finish the season off in South America before the finale in Abu Dhabi. The Grand Prix in Russia was cancelled due to the conflict between Ukraine and Russia.

Date	Grand Prix	Venue
20 March	Bahrain	Sakhir
27 March	Saudi Arabia	Jeddah
10 April	Australia	Melbourne
24 April	Emilia Romagna	Imola
8 May	Miami	Miami
22 May	Spain	Barcelona
29 May	Monaco	Monaco
12 June	Azerbaijan	Baku
19 June	Canada	Montreal
3 July	United Kingdom	Silverstone
10 July	Austria	Spielberg
24 July	France	Le Castellet
31 July	Hungary	Budapest
28 August	Belgium	Spa
4 September	Netherlands	Zandvoort
11 September	Italy	Monza
2 October	Singapore	Singapore
9 October	Japan	Suzuka
23 October	USA	Austin
30 October	Mexico	Mexico City
13 November	Brazil	Sao Paulo
20 November	Abu Dhabi	Abu Dhabi

HOW DO THEY DETERMINE WHO GETS WHICH GARAGE IN A RACE?

The team that wins the constructor championship in the previous season gets first pick on which garage they get at a grand prix. The second placed team gets second pick and so on. Next year it will be Mercedes first, then Red Bull, then Ferrari and Haas gets the remaining garage left after the rest of the teams picked.

WILL ANY RULES CHANGE REGARDING SAFETY CARS AND RACE CONTROL?

There is an ongoing investigation on what happened in Abu Dhabi, and it's likely that this situation will not repeat itself. Following the criticism from the teams to try and keep the race going but not giving anyone an advantage, it's likely that if there is a crash in the last couple of laps of a race, we will see a red flag and a race restart instead of a safety car.

WHY WAS SHAQUILLE O'NEILL SUDDENLY ON THE PODIUM?

Shaq was there to hand out the trophies and probably wanted to just enjoy the moment, so he stayed on the podium!

WHY DO PENALTIES FOR ENGINE CHANGES DIFFER PER DRIVER?

This may look like this happened in 2021, with Valteri getting a 5 grid penalty for his engine change and Max getting a full 20 grid penalty, but this doesn't depend on the driver but on the parts that are being changed. An F1 engine is made up of six different elements - the **Internal Combustion Engine (ICE), Turbo, MGU-K, MGU-H, Control Electronics and Energy Store**. These elements are combined together to deliver different Power Unit modes, which drivers and teams can utilise throughout a race weekend. At any race, a driver can choose to replace any part of the engine, which can result in a 5-grid penalty if you have exceeded the maximum part changes. However, if you change your full power unit (or too many components), you will receive a 20-grid penalty.

WHAT IS A SPEED TRAP?

A speed trap is one of those terms you hear all the time on TV and you will even see it come up as a visual quite frequently during the race and qualifying. It is actually a very important performance measure to **to detect the speed of the cars on track**. So the speed trap is a specific spot on the track where we can see the speed of the cars as they pass through this point. This allows us to compare the speed of the cars. While theoretically we can measure top speed of a car anywhere, you can probably imagine that it makes most sense to measure the top speed at the end of a long straight part of the track, as this is the part where a car will travel at the highest speed. However, this isn't the only place we see the speed trap occur. Another common place can be in the middle of a corner. Placing the speed trap at the middle of a corner gives us a good indication about which cars are taking the corners at a higher speed and which cars have to take the corners at a lower speed. While the speed trap doesn't reflect the full story of what is going on on track, it can be a good indication of which engines are performing better and which cars perform strongly in certain parts of the track. At the end of the day, the best indication is of course the stop watch. The stop watch never lies and a car that goes around the track fastest is the best car.

WHAT IS ARE TRACK SECTIONS AND WHAT DO THOSE COLOURS MEAN?

All tracks in Formula 1 are divided into three sections. This is done to give viewers and drivers an indication of how cars are performing in different parts of the track rather than just showing one big lap time. The tracks aren't necessarily divided into three equal thirds but rather into comparable parts of the track. We can take Monza as an example here. The first sector of Monza is a long straight, followed by a sharp turn and then another long straight. The second part is a part that consists of some medium turns following each other and the third sector is one long straight with a very long turn.

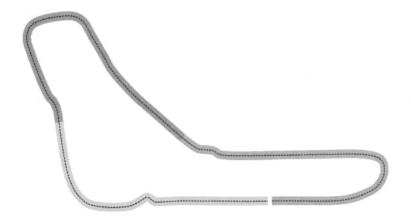

The colours that you will frequently see on TV all have a different meaning and are important to understand. There are 3 main colours that you can find on screen which are yellow, green and purple. Yellow indicates that a drive was slower in this sector than compared to his fastest lap. Green means that the driver has improved his own personal best time for that sector. Purple means the driver has set the fastest sector time of anyone during that session. What's important to understand is you can have three green sectors (so not purple) and still set the fastest time for a lap. As an example take these two drivers:

Sector	Driver A	Driver B	Driver C
1	23 seconds	22 Seconds	24 seconds
2	23 seonds	22 seconds	25 seconds
3	20 seconds	25 seconds	19 seconds
Lap Time	1:06	1:09	1:08

As you can see, driver A does not have any fastest sector times but still sets the fastest lap time. This is something to keep in mind when watching the qualifying and races as these sectors times are just indicators of how the drivers are doing but don't necessarily mean that a driver is going faster than another driver.

WHY ARE THERE THREE SPRINT RACES ? WHY NOT ALL SPRINT RACES?

Sprint races are new to Formula 1 and were only introduced in 2021. The new race format was introduced to make the sport more entertaining across the weekend rather than just on Sundays. Traditionally, Fridays were seen as pretty boring to watch for fans coming to the track. This is because you only saw Free Practice 1 and 2. With the sprint races, even Friday became an entertaining day to visit the track as Qualifying now takes place on Friday. The sport is still trialing this format of racing and therefore the race format only takes place over three race weekends. If the sprint races continue to be as spectacular as they have been in 2021, it could very well be possible that we will see an increase in these types of races.

HOW REALISTIC IS THE NETFLIX SERIES 'DRIVE TO SURVIVE'?

That's a good question! Of course, I don't have access to the paddock and private conversations of drivers either, so it's hard to assess. However, from what I see and hear from the drivers, it seems like the first season was reasonably realistic but as the series gained traction and popularity the show tried to get more dramatic and more over the top every season. This has led to the latest season (season 4) getting a lot of criticism from drivers as a lot of their comments have been taken out of context, and rivalries have been created that don't necessarily exist.

EPILOGUE

Hi there. It's me, Melvin. You got through every single page in this book and even made it to the epilogue! Amazing. I hope this book has been worth your time as this is the first book I've ever written. Its always been a dream of mine to write and publish my own book and you have made my dream come true by purchasing this book. If you have any feedback, leave a review, I'm a person who is always looking to learn and I hope this won't be the final book I write. I've spent hours and hours and hours learning and reading about Formula 1 even before writing this book and it gives me a lot of joy to be able to write all my thoughts down and share this knowledge with the world.

I'd like to thank my fiancé and my dad for reading through 72 pages of my thoughts and making me accountable to give the book structure, to make it well written and not a drag to read through. Enjoy the season, I'm sure it will be another one to look forward to